# Kat and Dan

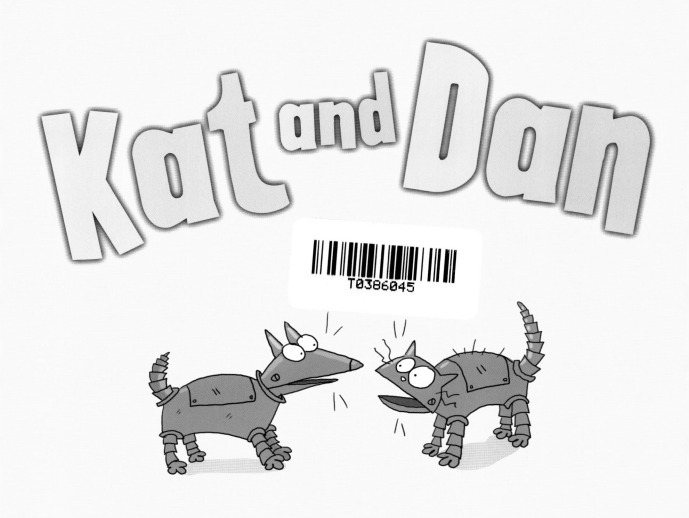

T0386045

Written by Monica Hughes

Illustrated by Joëlle Dreidemy

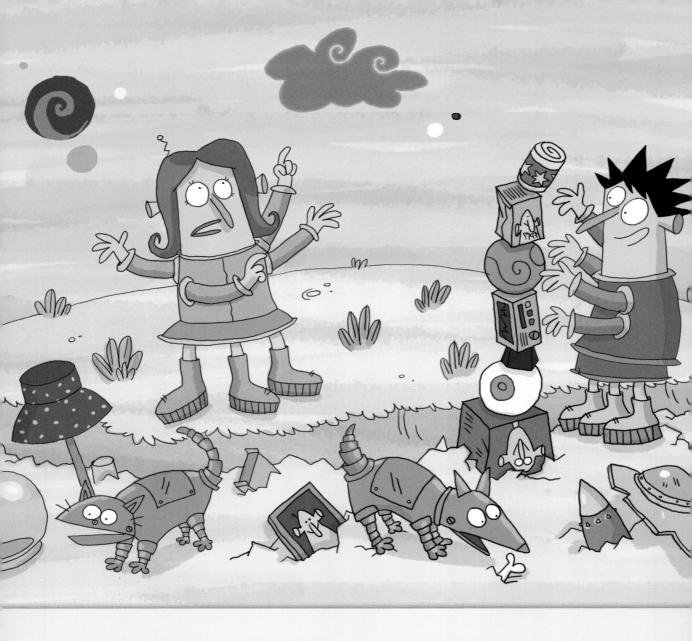

Kat and Dan nip to a tip.

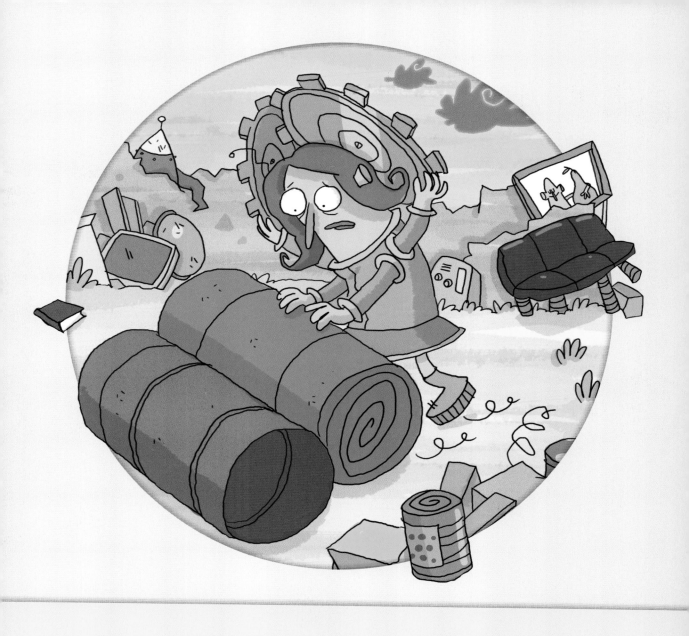

Kat got cans and cogs.

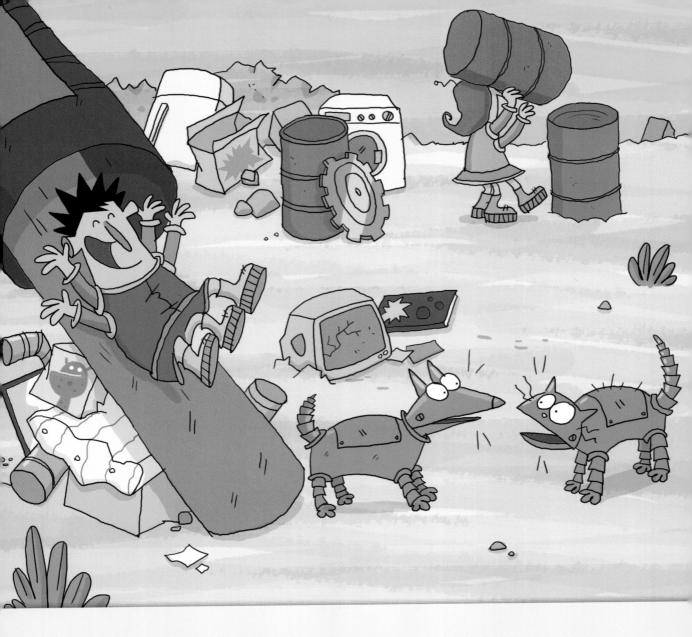

Dan did not.

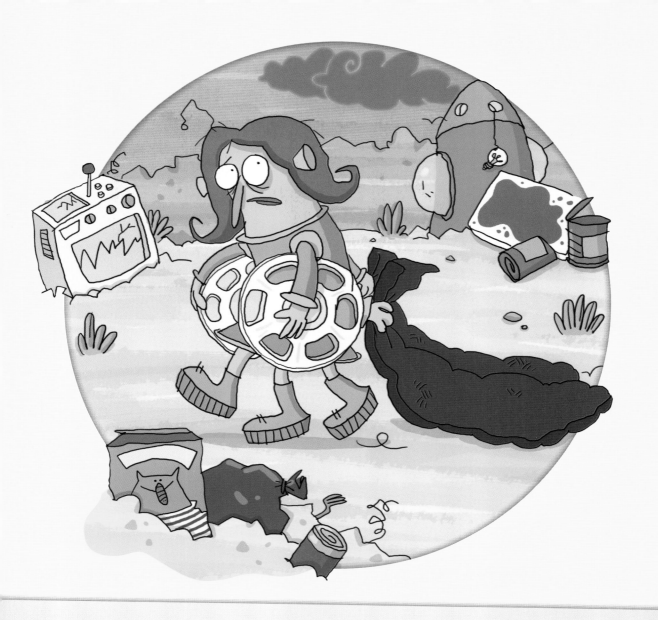

Kat got caps and mats.

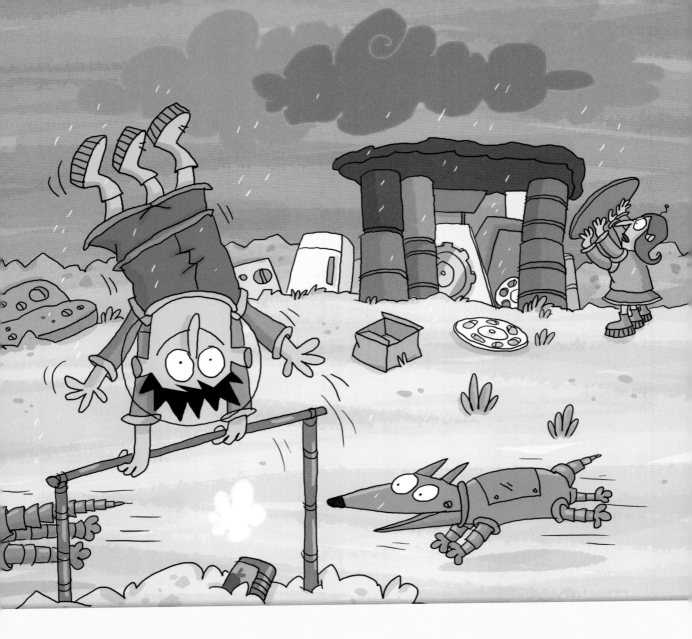

Dan did not.

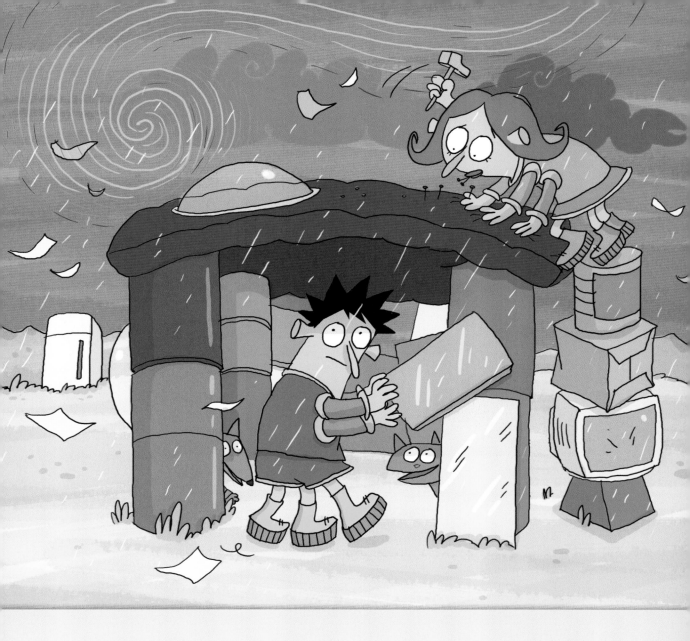

Dan got in.

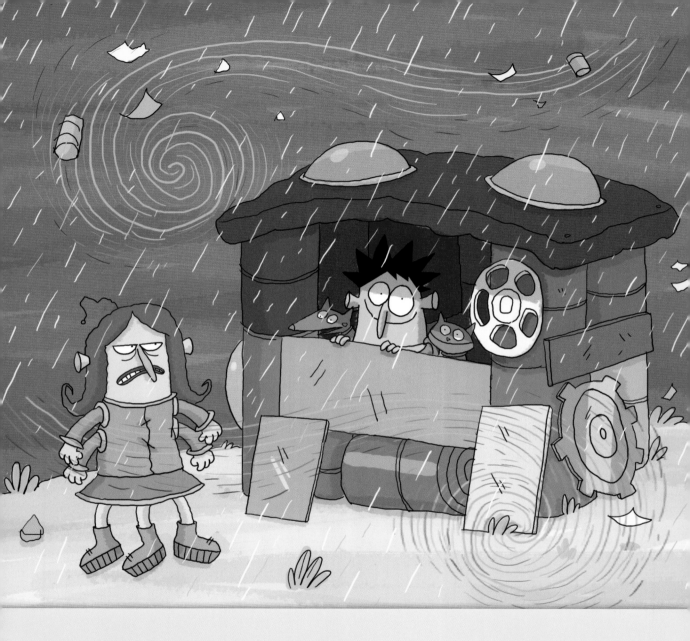

Kat did not!